# A Consecration of the Wind

### Selected Poems by
### Joanne Zarrillo Cherefko

Copyright 2018 © Joanne Cherefko

Supervising Editors: L. Austen Johnson, Camryn Nethken
Associate Editor: Sarah Pila

All rights reserved. No part of this publication may be reproduced, distributed, or transmitted in any form or by any means without the prior written permission of the publisher, except in the case of brief quotations and other noncommercial uses permitted by copyright law. For permission requests, write to publisher at Info@genzpublishing.org.

GenZPublishing.org
Aberdeen, NJ

ISBN: 9781723426018

"I will show you fear in a handful of dust."
                              T.S. Eliot

*Dedicated to my mother Frances, my Source,
and to my husband Bud, my Universe*

## TABLE OF CONTENTS

**The Art of Family** ............................................................................. 1
   Leaving Newark Behind ............................................................... 3
   First Fragments .............................................................................. 7
   The Man at the Window ............................................................... 8
   Second Fragments ........................................................................ 9
   Third Fragments .......................................................................... 10
   Money Tree ................................................................................... 11
   Survivor ......................................................................................... 12
   Michelle, A Gift of Life ................................................................ 13
   Bellows .......................................................................................... 14
   The Dream Twenty Years Later ............................................... 15
   Prelude .......................................................................................... 16
   Hazy Shades of 60s ..................................................................... 17
   Cherry Pits ................................................................................... 19
   Siblings ......................................................................................... 20

**The Art of Darkness** ....................................................................... 22
   Position Embracing Itself .......................................................... 24
   Twilight Windows ....................................................................... 26
   This Window is a Thirst but Not a Good Drink ................... 27
   Journey ......................................................................................... 29
   Zephyr II ....................................................................................... 30
   Divergent Paths .......................................................................... 31
   Invocations at Two and Three AM .......................................... 32
   Grim Images ................................................................................ 35
   Sighs That Become Real in Wombs of Glory ......................... 36
   Drowning Voices Once Awakened .......................................... 38
   Self and Lesser Images Twice Gleaned .................................. 39
   A Puff of Smoke .......................................................................... 41
   Into the Belly of the Monster ................................................... 42
   Configurations of a Third Glass of Wine ............................... 43
   Finite Blues .................................................................................. 44
   Surfaces ........................................................................................ 45

**The Art of Love** ................................................................................ 47
   Some Men I Have Known .......................................................... 49
   From Z to A .................................................................................. 50
   The Aftermath ............................................................................ 51
   Trolling at the Jersey Shore ..................................................... 52
   How Well Do You Read My Eyes? ........................................... 54

| | |
|---|---|
| Renegade | 55 |
| Swimming Alphabetically in the Years Before Bud | 56 |
| Budding | 59 |
| Mah Jongg, Vodka, and Bud | 60 |
| Bud | 61 |
| My Husband | 62 |
| Folds | 63 |
| Love Then and Now | 64 |
| **The Art of Places** | **66** |
| Tangier | 68 |
| On the Return from Italy to Paris | 69 |
| High Bridge | 70 |
| The Other Grand Canyon | 71 |
| On the Road to Mann Lodge | 72 |
| Cedar Run Inn | 73 |
| Tennessee Wind Farm | 74 |
| Reflections in a Blue High-Rise | 75 |
| Gina I, II, III | 76 |
| Mono Lake | 78 |
| Yosemite from Ansel's Lens | 79 |
| "La Rochelle 1896" | 80 |
| "Venetian Patina" | 81 |
| Bubbles Trail | 82 |
| Full Circle Farmhouse | 84 |
| Fish Pond | 85 |
| Browntown Valley | 86 |
| The Glow | 87 |

# The Art of Family

**Leaving Newark Behind**

The musty smell of moisture-laden
Cotton and wool upholstery
In 50's sedans
Produces an irrational
Revulsion...
Perhaps it was the
Motion sickness while
Listening to "Three Little Fishies"
Playing on the radio,
The smoke from
My parents' L&M's, and
My father's press and release
Of the gas pedal again and again
For no apparent reason
On the ride from Middletown
To Manahawkin.
Sitting forward and opening the window
Did not prevent the release
Of gastric remnants
Along the Parkway.

A certain preacher on TV
Provoked revulsion too.
Why this man of God
Sent me reeling and running
In fear was a mystery.
For decades, I thought someone like him
Was the architect of my nightmares,
Until the family picnic
When secrets unknowingly buried
Poked through the surface
Of membranes to pierce my skull.

My unknowing had painted a portrait that
Vanished under scrutiny.
The knowing must be that
My parents left Parker Street
To own a house in the suburbs,
Like other families who formed

An exodus from cities
Once cars became the norm
And the GI bill, the prize.

The knowing must be that
The butcher on the corner
Was stabbed, and my parents were afraid.
There was a shootout in our backyard,
And my parents were afraid.
Men with machine guns went into
The warehouse on Garside Street,
Across from Aunt Rosie's place,
And my parents were afraid.
The long walk down a dark hall
With curtains concealing scary monsters,
And the stern-faced aunt at the end of the hall
In a kitchen that smelled of pepper and egg
Sandwiches in olive oil stained bags
Was what scared me.

And then, while 7, 6, and 5,
Barbara, Janice, and I
Played on the sidewalk while two
Heavily-bodied, smiling strangers
Approached us on the street,
Offering Janice candy in exchange for a ride,
And our parents were afraid.

At the picnic 30 years later
I started the conversation
About the men, my cousin,
The sedan, and the candy.

Janice looked at me curiously,
But my sister's response was
Unexpected,
Shocking,
Revelatory.
I was the one offered the candy;
I was the one heading for the car
Until my sister and cousin

Stopped me,
Saving my life,
Or so they said.

I denied their shared memory
Until their raised voices
Blended in harmony
To tell me my past was a lie,
My memory, a hoax.

It would take years to untangle
The slender strand of thought
That drifted
From knowing to unknowing.
There was no trauma
In the memory of candy
Or a ride offered by
Smiling gentlemen in suits.
There was, on the surface,
No trauma deeply suppressed,
And yet, the aroma of cars
And a preacher's likeness
Held secrets.

The epiphany, late in arrival,
Suddenly pierced the membrane
That shielded the idea of it,
Though I'm not sure of its truth.
The trauma of aromas
And the preacher's likeness
Didn't come from the offer on the street.
It was borne of the dissociative union
Of frightened parents and lessons
To be learned by a little girl.
Well-meaning guardians,
Afraid of the darkness on the streets,
Assaulted my sense of being
And excised the event
Into the place of unknowing.

After the picnic, the preacher's image
Ceased to cause a reaction;
He was now indistinguishable
From any man of any size or face,
No longer the symbol of a looming monster
Of which suppressed dreams are made.
But the smell of old sedans
Still has a visceral effect.
I guess that has more to do with
Listening to 40s songs
And gagging on secondhand smoke
While waiting for my father to pull over
So I could purge and pause
The ceaseless back and forth
Of his foot on the pedal.

**First Fragments**

When ten and five years
Crashed down on my
Well-trodden soul,
I found refuge in
Autumnal backyards
Where landscapes
Were as barren
As those eyes
That saw
Sad, empty branches
Bent with empathetic
Shadows over ice
Where our cat
Froze one winter
And where her sister
Always nobly sat
On the diving platform.

The lack of leaves
Inspired me;
My dark thoughts
Were justified,
God had
Failed some of us
In Middletown,
And no buses
Stopped here
To provide flight
For captive souls
Or to alter that
Bleak backyard
Scenario that
Absorbed my agony
In its bare, brown bones.

**The Man at the Window**

A black and green
Hand-me-down bikini
With two ties that knotted
At the center of
My developing chest
Was all that covered
My white, supple body
As I lay in the back yard,
Shading my eyes
From the figure at the window.

The only motion to disrupt the stillness
Came when that imperfect outline of a man
Slithered through the humid midday air
To stand in the hot sun
And gaze at my figure
While holding the hose
On the velvety cockscomb.

**Second Fragments**

He smelled of
Many summers past
And still perspired
Through winters
Of sectioning
Sunday papers
Later piled
In the back of
A blue station wagon
And thrown
From the car window
At homes that inspired
Envy and shame.
Eyes other than his
Viewed those houses
And widened
In the act of viewing.
Those same such eyes
Rode next to
His on trucks
That rang out
And offered
Ice delights
To children
Who screamed
Profanities and rode
Back bumpers.
Those were our times
Together, not spent
In familial love, but
In as much closeness
As could be had
Amid violent seas
Besieged by
Hate and pity.

**Third Fragments**

The light
Came down on
Each scene.
Though not
Angled from
The skies, down
It came,
Wrenching out
Of my pores
The agony that
Ripped apart
My insides.
This light
Came out of her
Brown eyes
That enveloped me
With their suffering
Voice and solace
Buried in limbs.
This sad sunlight
Was my release,
My only warmth
In a sea of autumns
And wintry interiors,
But it was shaded
From me just when
My winters ceased
To be.

**Money Tree**

As summer eclipsed,
She peeled the
Sides of the flowers
And saved the seeds
In an envelope.

She arranged the money trees
In bottles, vases, and jars
And gave them to
Her family and friends
Before she died.

The fibrous leaves hang,
Their veins shade beige to brown,
Their stems crisscross
In the bottle
And press against the glass.

So lovely, this gift
She left before she died.

**Survivor**

Give death to the wailing wall;
It breeds monsters within me
That cannot control themselves,
As though tears could penetrate
The membrane between
Sensation and cessation.

Pieces of me break off and
Re-associate themselves
And flow into melodies
That strain my memory.
I have a vision of hugging
And kissing my mother.
I have a dream
That this is a dream.

To be alive is to die, but
I will never master
The ability to say goodbye.

**Michelle, A Gift of Life**

From her fragile eyes
All of my tomorrows flowed
Like a gentle surge of music.

Through her, I became
Whole by a soft
Diffusion of images
And a sacrifice of memories.

Looking through her eyes,
I saw the possibility
Of viewing life
Without pain and regret.

She became the
New and improved One
From whom our mingled
Waters flowed—
        Sometimes red, becoming clear,
        Always baptismal in quest,
        Yet muddy with denial
        Of those rocks that
        Rose toward my face
        As I tried to stay above water.

She was the first
Who became the river
That flowed gently through
My dark caverns
And saved me from drowning.

**Bellows**

A frightening dream it was
As we found our place
In a darkened cathedral
Where a frail woman in white lace
Was being kept alive.
Religiously, they pumped bellows
Into her body.
"Slowly; you must do it slowly,
Or the rush of air shall kill her!"
And I recognized her.
This thin, half-shadow person
Was my mother,
And in a moment
She died before my eyes.
I feared it
I escaped it
But finally
It embraced me.

**The Dream Twenty Years Later**

Finally, one night
My mother forgave me
And hugged me
As only she could.
I sat upright in bed
After her soul
Went through my body
Like a tornado,
But it was too late to traverse
Those cavernous tunnels
That led to her.
She had become so weakened
By her own strength of emotion
That she was lost to me forever.

**Prelude**

The tremulous thought
Was thrust into reality,
And I temporarily
Became sanctified
When she died.
The hole in me
Widened to absorb
My agony in spasms
As I flashed back and
Wanted to envelop
Her whole life,
To be her friend when
She was a child,
But I was forty years too late
To become holy
Through a vision,
And was she really
Ever a child?  Or
Did those visions lie?

And now I have blossomed
Through the release
Her death has wrought,
Though I will always
Be borne back again
To peer from
Wombs down uncertain
Corridors in discovery
And subsequent
Shedding of self.
In my saner moments
I feel protected
From the abyss,
But I always wither
And leave part of me
Behind, hanging
From the precipice,
Just in case this world
Gets too much with me.

**Hazy Shades of 60s**

I remember the 60s well
So I was not
Part or whole of it—
No drug-infused haze
No alcohol
No high school parties
No boyfriends after
Fourth grade…
Only memories of
Rich girls from the
"Right side" of Highway 35
In plaid skirts
And wool sweaters
Bought in expensive shops
In Red Bank.
I wore my sister's discards
And polyester from a bleak
Grocery store located on
The other side of cool.

But the music…
The music…
I still remember each lyric
And I still feel each note.
Vicariously, I lived through the
Rebellion of Dylan and Baez,
The haunting melodies of Simon
And Garfunkel,
But I preferred Motown to Folk
Because I couldn't gyrate to
"Sounds of Silence"
Strummed on an acoustic guitar.

I didn't protest
The Vietnam War
Because I didn't understand it
Until I was in my 60s.
Then I put it in perspective
With all wars

Ordained by
"Janus-faced" politicians
Who bless and deny
Acceptable loss.

I blame my absenteeism
From the 60s
On my unwillingness
To peek beyond
My mother's pious shadow.

**Cherry Pits**

Clusters of cherry pits
Richly tan in the center
And framed by mushy burgundy
Form patterns
In the empty plastic container.

The clusters remind me of
Wasp nest cells—
Open half-circles
Forming blotches
That block my vision.

What Freudian dream
Fostered that revulsion?
Was it the tripe
My mother used to boil on the stove?
I have no recollection of taste,
Only the putrid aroma of
Cellular intestinal walls
That drove me out of the house.

But these are just cherry pits
With stems connecting
The patterned cells,
No dreams
No aromas
Just a red stain on my teeth
Ruining my imperfect smile
During the aftermath of a
Mid-summer rainstorm.

**Siblings**

Two athletes and a guitar player
All took different paths in life,
Loved differently
And settled in different places.
Did each suffer the pangs of
Self-awareness and regret?
No one can say for sure.

But each developed
A personalized style of
Tucking and rolling away from
The darkest moments.
Did they stick the landing?
Who knows?

Now they view their blended history
With three sets of eyes and aging hearts,
Remembering the familiar
In foreign ways,
Each holding a magnifying glass
Delicately balanced over
Decades of thread
Woven from half-told truths.
Will the seams hold?
No one can tell.

They exhale separate lives of
Noisy desperation
That overlap on those
Special celebratory moments
When they compare notes
About failing body parts.
Who suffers the most?
No one knows.

But they survived their father's life
And their mother's death
And now they each live in pain,
Serving penance as the offspring
Of a misconceived notion.

# The Art of Darkness

**Position Embracing Itself**

I have seen your face
Among other faces
Until you, undisguised,
Fade into the mist.
Then the images become
Blurred upon appearance.
The boardwalk, empty,
Emerges with the tide,
And shells left unturned
Bleed rhythmically
With the waves.
A shallowness of horizons unstirred
Comes running to me.

Swaddled in November,
Buried under snow,
An apparition appeared
And disappeared on course
Like soft music flowing
From a Muse's hands and eyes.
First the eyes blinked,
Then the veins became exposed.
In the fountain,
Water spuming from her mouth,
She stands still,
Oblivious to the wet eyes.

Night,
Alone with the whispering smoke
Of a figure abreast of me,
The saccharine fumes of it
Running across my shoulders,
Blurring my vision of trees
Staggering before me,
Of smoke
Curling between my legs.
As daylight broke
The landscape into colors,
I left a piece of flesh

Behind to turn to ashes.

Rocking
And watching the patterns
Of snow on the pane,
They melt and merge
Till beyond them
I see your face.
We acknowledge sighs
And separate breaths,
And you sense the duality
That occurs within me.
Later, when you are one
With the horizon,
I smell your skin
As though you were still here.

Out of the fog
Summer is born, and
The artifice of love has surfaced.
I have been in the car
Careening down the road
Till the fear of the impact
Brought me back.
Outside, the lightning strikes
A sensual blow,
But the storms occur
In the wombs of women.

A consecration of the wind
In a tawny month reveals
Images that flicker and return
To disrupt, while
Words drift numbly and vanish
Before the dropping of a rose.
In the stillness, the breeze
Encounters a shadow.
A pale fume writhes its way
Through the earth;
I will not surface again...
I will not surface.

**Twilight Windows**

Brows that lean from windows
Are cast in wonder inside
A thousand lonely rooms.

Eyes that linger in shadows
Beckon strands of light
From dusty sills
Where she gazes,
Shirtsleeves raised slightly
To permit the diffusion of light
From distant portals.

Starless, she wonders at
The rampant whirl of emotion
Caught below in timeless exposure
As she bemoans her
Collection of chairs,
Disarming and still in
These twilight scenes.

Lint drifts from her
As light traces the pattern
In the air that swirls
Her in a raptureless cocoon.

**This Window is a Thirst but Not a Good Drink**

From this window
In time and space,
I mark my place
With the soft
Retreat of senses
And a slow dance to
Self and lessness.
Below, pale offerings
Emerge from sun caverns to
Delight the sidewalks.

From a Hopper-lit
Soft corner of
A window
I see faces,
Distorted and stretched
To screams of
Sad orifices that
Used to delight
Sidewalk persons.

I prefer this
Downward view
Shaded by drawn,
Sanctimonious pillars
That split this curtain
On fateful or frivolous
Occasions that have
Marked my place
In time and space.

Having no more truths
I can deny to myself,
I ask my monsters
To surrender,
To come inside the window, and
Not to shatter those images of

Cardboard people
Marking places
In other times
Through uncertain faces
And switched spaces
Of light from
Former windows.

**Journey**

A quizzical figure
Slanted between frozen angles of suggestion
Leans against mirrors that reverse themselves
To caverns at once sacred and savage.
This feminine outline, perfect and shaded,
Avoids her reflection in the churning waters below,
Revealing only misdirection in these dark passages...

A soft figure that fills itself to the given space
And releases its parts to the air upon suggestion
Retreats from outlines imperfect in melting glass.

These maze-ridden paradoxes seem to converge
At various surface parts
Or rather the mirrors suggest such a cavernous union
That closed eyes cannot deny...

To see the other as if for the first time
Is the journey of seeing myself at the last expanse,
The final seascape of bleeding crustacea
Beckoning my feet already partially cleansed
By waters running through me to your break.

**Zephyr II**

Distant landscapes fold
Into shores of memory
Where gazers glide to greet
This mistress to an understatement.
She circumvents pebbles and roots
That surface during low tide
And morph into
Ideas and words that
Reflect ovarian platitudes,
Forming blinders
Over her eyes that
Smile inwardly
At rough surfaces.
The woman and her shadow,
Both as indiscrete figures,
Walk across the grain
Of symbolic overtures
To points that rise
To meet the expanse.
Layers of color bleed
From the circle and erase
Images etched from the sea,
Uniting and dividing
The two at once
In a languid waltz of fluid thought
Where people other than I have bathed
In waters stagnant with resolve.

**Divergent Paths**

Her horizontal landscape,
Series of electrical switches
And bulbs blinking,
Flickers until all is
Dark inside the cave.
From walls shadowless and sublime
Two voices emerge
In correspondence,
Deflecting light vestiges that
Pour in columns through her skin.
Words rain softly
In converging nuances
And muted echoes whose reach
Is each to each
Until harsher light
Permeates her circuitry.
Then throats scream, parched from
Dry eggshells that bleed
Betrayals and swim
Through dark, cavernous ruins
Where words skip through
Veiny tunnels
Of dry thoughts.
The cacophony of soul catchers
Lingering outside these walls
Reaches silent ears that are
Caught in an embrace
Of former fears
In a frenzied journey
To that improved translation
Of endings.

## Invocations at Two and Three AM

My youth passes from my sides,
Startled into scattered crystals
That blow from me
Like blue goblets
When winds bearing mindless words
Cut through the decorum of smiles,
And I realize that I alone
Am my shadow beside me.

Fold me so these silent
Screams cannot echo,
But be absorbed
And distilled into release
When I, unfolded,
Melt back to me
And greet the dichotomous foe.

Breathe me into being real
To become unreal again
Through forces
Whispered through my pores.
I emerge from these pages
As distinct half-notes
Of ashes that I left behind
In traces with
No uncertain pattern,
Afraid to claim this world as
My own design.

Give me whispered flows
That know not me
And purge in denial of themselves.
All this to become real
And less, much less.

Fragments return to
Create a mist
Before new immersions
Which must release

Themselves into this air
Of corners where
I rather let the
Night take me,
And let the words
Read to me my scope
Of horror, buried
In stately tombs of disarray
Among costumed mourners
Whose countenance
Is one shadow of lies.

I dissipate and scatter my crystals
On these meek pages;
I stand between and
Around each letter
And know not if
I support them or they, me
Or if this symbiotic
Turn is horizontal
Or vertical betrayal of self,
And if I will remain castigated
By lower-case platitudes
Turned profound around
My four o'clock blues.

Section me so
My pieces are smooth
And lay me on
The ashes of this bed
Whereon all but
The shells have died
And await renewal.

Take me and bury me again
Until I blossom clean to write
The breath of startled images
And the death of those
Whose rustling
Is but a shadow
From a dream sequence.

Then set me to a rhythm
Which omits notes
Once removed from being
And make me the song
That whispers through
These morphemes.
Make me graphic
And the analysis complete
To release only the feel.

Sounds slide and letters bleed
From my wounds.
They hurl themselves onto the
Pyre, making
Immortal only the smoke
And ashes of what
They might have been
And what I will never be,
Trapped inside
These charred ruins
Of templed faces.

**Grim Images**

From the edge, I see
A progression of revolving faces
Swirled in smoke from a thousand
Fragmented rooms...
Faces that overwhelm these
Breathed-through walls
With a satisfied perplexity...
My heart races for
A face that withdraws
From this scene
Where shades of doubt
Drape walls of fear
In a seemingly distant
Rapport of rapturous souls...
In my mind, I am not there;
I am not part of a loving pair
In these rooms that are bracketed and bare.
Amid this revolution of Friday night faces
Prepared for such perplexity,
I scan each horizon to scale
And move into a new, but
Not too distant corner,
Looking back in self-dismay
To a day when rooms
Will be satisfactorily peopled,
And I, less symbolically arranged.

**Sighs That Become Real in Wombs of Glory**

There is, within this scheme,
A monochromatic vision
A circumcision
Of moments, thoughts,
And whispers that
Relent to the frowns and sighs
Of bodies swept by visions
Not of plums or of fairies
But of Bergman landscapes,
Of a grey, desperate acceptance.
Who will claim
This body that has been
Assaulted by such visions?
As though to take the sighs
Out of those souls
And to see them
For the first time
In death
Would do for want
Of something more.

Words fade before
Succeeding to
Make one reel
With the feel of them,
But they glow with
Tragic openings and closures;
They glide with a sense
Of lost meaning
And glimmer through
Bits of thoughts
That came in depths
Of dreams and dissipated
At dawn.

In winter and in snow,
We go down.
In sickness and in health,
We go. We descend to our
Beginnings and know
Them to be the ends
And ways of going,
Of becoming unreal
To truly feel and flow
In this particular light.
So I pass through this mirror
To see you broken by it.
You decide when you will glide
Down to meet me
In angular delusion.
I will remain here,
Blanketed by my
Own confusion and
Loss of self,
Having passed
It through former
Frames of glass,
Through soft cries
Of aborted humor
And ghostly hows and whys.

She should have
Cut this cord years ago,
But she always journeys down,
Cushioning her falls
With warm, uterine walls.

**Drowning Voices Once Awakened**

A familial sigh,
Provoked and sustained
By fire and water shells
And their respective
Fragmented passions,
Is euphemized
To a safely distant regard
For my being
As long as I not be too am.

Dealing in such subterfuge,
These statuesque waterways
Undermine
All of my rhetorical devices.
And so, too, do I deal
In ice and try with my skin
To make ethereal
These glass surfaces.

Thrust into the abysmal chill,
Embryonic tears melt the voices
That seep through walls
In shadows
And laugh at their
Consciousness of fate.

Lacking what to do
With fire once reached,
I prepare my own shell
To greet
The embers that I meet
In similitude.
These singular stalks of ice
Stand violated by
Water and fire's flow,
Their shadowy silhouettes
Submerged in sighs
I left behind.

## Self and Lesser Images Twice Gleaned

The cycle of looking at familiar scenes
Resumes itself in different tones.
Visions occur and
Confuse a soul
That presumes to know
What has been seen before.

These curious moments
Return to one now engaged
In twilight hues
Of a spring evening languor
That recalls no winters of despair.
Each picture, stilled from
Different passages, conveys
An image as such we
Will never see again
From this mean.

I sail quietly
Amid these scenes;
From this chair I move
To uncertain spaces
Caught between poetic lines
Of self-renewal
And a mirrored image
That moves me to tears,
Infinite and gentle,
Not to be shared
With friends whose
Souls conform to unfamiliar rhythms.

A vision I defer
Is lost momently,
Only to reappear in
My dreams as a
Vestige of nonchalance,
Of timorous skin movements
Betrayed by self-denial.

Let this malady flow
Through portals sacrificed
To meaningful gestures
Thrust from effigies
Whose eyes reveal a soul
That has yet to be filled.

I return, meanwhile,
To familiar notions
Of a green-cushioned complacency
Born of muted
Black and white portraits
And a beige aura of well-being.
In doing so, I bid an end
To friends whose souls are fixed
In a sensory ear.

**A Puff of Smoke**

A twist of lemon, bitter and cool,
Bites me where I subvocalize;
Fragments of straw cluttered with dung
Are left for me to analyze.
As I twist the lemon and step on the dung,
I render my fate to time;
When clouds clutter the sky,
Bitter and cool,
I go from lemon to lime.

**Into the Belly of the Monster**

Into the belly of the monster,
The journey of
The first passing,
She drove
    Through the cooling twilight
    Where she defined herself
    Amid viscera
    And skeletal remains—
    Off-white structures
    That signaled the path
    To the center, primordial chord
    That, when plucked,
    Would resound earthly tremors.

Ominous tusks lie entwined with
Vitreous portions of bulging
Eyelids and black, huddled forms
Within this huge, indefinable something.

This blank space took on a lifeless
And amorphous form,
A navigable, vague river
Contorting through the grey matter.

## Configurations of a Third Glass of Wine

The recognition comes softly
On a wet palpitation
To a face poised in pristine
Glass views.
Surreal figures
Dance between
Visceral rhythms
And nocturnal whisperings
Upon the portent
Of a synthetic urge.
As the literary quarter-note
Sways itself to spondaic
Death or surmise,
I begin and end
As a solitary figure
Rising from the expanse...
Such a unity is hardly
Imposed over another
Fragmented night.

**Finite Blues**

Finite blues
Cross my mind
Like razor blades
Splitting my eyeballs.
I have fractured
Me again,
So I press my remains
Hard against my mattress,
Bruising and begging
Sleep.
Then
I jump back
Out of that body
And look on
In abandonment
While a conductor
In my head
Plays against a wall of music,
Trying to stop it
Or blur it into abstraction
And woo me to sleep.

**Surfaces**

Three levels below
All of my morphemes
Lies the meaning
I impart to myself.

Rules of prosody
And years of Eliot
Lend real art
To my lies;
They serve as coverlets
For naked breasts
And gaping orifices.

Words are draped about me,
Shelved inside me
On reusable type,
And are liquefied to
Infinitely acceptable platitudes...
Not quite trite
And not at all true.

Come judgment day
I hope to belie
My former appearances
And hide behind
New letters and forms,
All but spared
From revelation.

# The Art of Love

**Some Men I Have Known**

As we converse, I see
Lines coming from you
And entering me at angles.
Red flashes of innuendos
Cushioned by blue dots
Bounce off corners
To return to the point of
Beginning. I ask why,
And know the answer
To be in the question itself,
And know the numbing to be
The result of angular collusion.
To feel that the cold
Will be softened by
Future caresses does not
Lessen the distance
Between two points converging.
Knowing that the beginning
Is my end, I ventilate
All dusty rooms and
Aerate all porous groans
To once again
Be consumed by them
Just as they free me.
You ask why
And know not
That the answer lies
In your geometry of being.

**From Z to A**

As evening lays
Its opaque shroud over us,
I am aware of the shadow
Of silence between us.
Yesterday's fantasy
Is today's demise
And the future
Lends itself to compromise.
The swift water of summer
Stagnates in the October mist,
The strength of old words
Withers in Autumn's fist.
I am a progression
On whose procession
It rained,
So the shroud, the shadow
And I leave, drained.

**The Aftermath**

When the train is gone,
When the sound
That pierced the distance
Becomes one with the distance
And is gone,
What is left?

When the tremulous earth
Is stilled,
When the quake
That consumed me
Is consumed by the horizon,
What is left?

When the image
Is only a memory,
When the fury
That shattered your skull
Is shattered and tamed
In one breath,
What is left
But the two of us?

Gazing at the aftermath
Of steel and smoke
I am content to feel nothing
And everything,
For the energy between us
Is enough
To bring the train back.

**Trolling at the Jersey Shore**

As disco stool ghouls
We awaited Mr. Right
At Jersey Shore bars
And listened to live bands
As our chests vibrated
From the sound
Of Morrison and Joel covers
Blaring from large speakers
On the dance floor.

At the Ship Wheel Inn
We got free drinks
So I poisoned my palate
With cheap vodka
And watered-down orange juice
To blur my expectations.

Only when the lights came on
At the transformed Inn
At 2 AM did we notice
The grime and
Stale smell
Of beer-soaked dirty rugs,
But we were young
And didn't need dim lighting
To fuel the interest
Of males in the rut.

Afterwards, the drive
To OB diner in Point Pleasant
Was an erratic jaunt
To caloric sobriety
As we assessed the looks
The dance moves
The lines
And the availability of men
Who claimed they weren't married.

Radar improved each Friday night
As we approached 30
And found ourselves alone.

Despite the hustle
We sought perspired bodies
To be next to
Eyes to meet
And golden idols
Falling from barstools
To catch.

**How Well Do You Read My Eyes?**

I must pluck
Out of my eyes
The revealing mist
Of flutters
I feel
When I conjure you,
To remain whole
And removed
In cushions
Of dark solitude.

Forgive me,
But this is a notional line
Over which a leap
Would bury me under.

Bases, however drifting,
Are attached to
Umbilical chords
Of sad love instrumentals,
So I resist and keep holy
Some memory of motion
And preserve you and me
While strengthening
What is between us.

And yet I flutter,
Muttering apologies
To empty chairs.

**Renegade**

I am driven over by you;
My heart fibrillates
Then contemplates itself
Into normalcy.
I try to be so sane,
So removed from you, and
Unaware of your poetic form,
But I have scanned and plotted
And swayed and stressed
In soft anapests
With you.
Your blood pours into my veins
And I glance out
From behind your eyes.
I shudder
With the flow of our
Moving, interchangeable parts,
But you see the me
That I pretend to be
So to remain,
You must never
Peer beyond the flap
Of nonchalance
Created to counter
Every move your soul makes
Toward mine.

**Swimming Alphabetically in the Years Before Bud**

C was her first tidal surge.
She let him
Decide the course of their
Intermingled waters.
She edited his papers
And he revised her view of love.
She never noticed the grey cloud
That hovered over her
While she was "in love,"
But it disappeared the moment
He wanted to "see others"
Along with her
(He uttered after
Her final editing job.)
She let her lungs exhale
After a long, submerged breath
And pulled the plug,
Draining his shallow
Pool of water.

B was her second surge.
She let him also
Decide the flow of their
Intermingled waters
And joined his search to find
Insulators at a railroad station
In Casper, Wyoming.
She watched water form in his eyes
As he described
The home they would share
In Binghamton, NY.
She felt secure
When he dropped his other girl
Until he dropped her too.
Then she fantasized
About a reunion at Montclair,
And the note on the car from
The young man behind the tree
Renewed her hope

Until he broke her heart
A final time.
Afterwards
Her mother said,
"It would never have worked."
She became angry
    What did her mother know
    Of the depths of their love?
She raged until
She sought her reflection
In the water.
Her mother was right;
The quick-tempered, profane
Dancing girl was gone.
In his pond,
Her image had disappeared altogether.

D was the swirling vortex
She met in a guidance office,
A friend of a friend.
She couldn't see
Where his shore and her
Sea foam met, but still
He said "I love you"
Before her waters began to rise.
Only after the roar
Of his F-15 subsided
Was she able to say it back.
He grimaced, defining "love"
As spontaneous and momentary,
Nothing to take too seriously.
But he kept floating around
And she foolishly thought
She could handle casual
Until she couldn't,
So she removed her toes
Before the high tide came in.

The moon controlled
Her ebb and flow,
Allowing her insecurities

And their betrayals
To comingle,
Or she would have settled
For a letter,
Remaining submerged
Beneath murky waters.

At the exact moment
She felt her own waves
Beginning to crest,
She fell for a guy
She met in a bar
Six years before.
Bud let her
Teach him how to swim
In the blood
Coursing through her veins,
In the waters
Flowing through her depths.
He loved her fluidity,
Despite knowing
How dark and blue
And unpredictable
Her waterways were,
And how susceptible they were
To lightning and hail.

**Budding**

A summer cold
Clouds my normally
Cerebral whimsy;
I feel romantic
With no one here
To share
What romantics share.
Intimacies nestle themselves within
While, without him, I grasp effigies
And plan cathartic scenes
That will never be played,
However intricately rehearsed
They may be.
Were he to feel
What I now feel,
My ragged edges
Would soften and
Cradle themselves
Within my scarred interior.
A perfection of the flesh,
Sacred and savage at once,
Pleads to elongate the moment's flight.

**Mah Jongg, Vodka, and Bud**

As you were
Kissing
And touching me
It became clear
That each motion
Each rush and
Each way we
Positioned ourselves
In respect to each other
Had its counterpart
In Mah Jongg configurations.
For one moment, we were
A progression of 5 7 9 bams;
When you were beside me
I experienced fours and eights.
It made so much sense
It was frightening,
How we fit into the patterns and
How they fit into my life.
I wonder which winds
Will take us to flowers
Or if the joker will have us after all.
While I fade into 3's turning to 6's and 9's
Think of you and me as like numerals.

**Bud**

He softens my corners;
>Even in this moment
>Of severe angles, he
>Encircles me.
What sacrifice would tell?
What kiss would reveal
>That inside
>I have borne him;
>That within
>He has created me;
>That without,
>I am not?

**My Husband**

As I lower myself onto
Your surface
I am borne back again inside
The face of a little girl,
Staring in awe
At what was once forbidden
And foreboding.

But now, you allay
All fear
As you draw me back to you
And weave me into your fabric,
Releasing my demons
To the air.

Touching you renders
And transports me
To unearthly delights.
As your lips graze mine
My cavernous walls crumble,
Permitting the heavens
To enter.

You have brought
Light to darkness
And life
To a dying embrace.
You give voice to the silent
Desires of my heart
And religion
To the emptiness of my soul.

**Folds**

A succession of faces
Embedded
Within the folds of
Your smile
Calls forth
Past embraces
And wonder
Through door crevices.

Cell-like structures
Become webs,
Tiny strands
Of molecular miracles
That cross my face.

The cocoon, once
Raptureless, now
Enfolds us in a
Slow dance
Of sheer joy
And subtle
Palpitations.

You have been inside me
From the moment
Of my conception.
You are my past
And my future,
My altar
And the religion
That thunders through this purgatory
Of passion.

**Love Then and Now**

Love in the First Year

In that first year,
Broken from fated liaisons
Bereft of hope
And still bleeding
From my mother's death,
I used to awaken
Startled to see him
Beside me.
I thought that our relationship
Was just a dream,
That happiness could not possibly
Be real for me -
I was surprised
And overwhelmed by our love.

Love in the 35th Year

In my dreams, he disappoints,
Frustrates, betrays
And I rage (no surprise).
Awakening with ire
I name his sins
And he laughs
Finding me strange
Not taking me seriously;
Why would he?

During the day
I still rage,
Screaming at deaf ears and
Awaiting tortoise-like reactions
From an old man with flat-line emotions,

And he still laughs
At an old woman,
An erratic edge of myopic sorrow
With earthquake emotions.

I am still surprised
And overwhelmed
By our love,
And I am glad that when I awake
He is still beside me.

# The Art of Places

**Tangier**

There is a view in Tangier
    That travels through trees
        Onto the variegated blue bay waters.
I have seen that view in another place,
    Through a lens that equally distorts.
This is the rebirth of the first edition
    *Tender is the Night* Scribner cover.
So I try to recall the tenderness of Tangier
The dry desert air, the sandaled feet
    That raised dust in the market place,
The dealers, snake charmers,
Bargain hunters, camel riders,
The six-fingered tailor who offered
    Couscous to the starving Americans,
The hole in the floor and the bucket of water,
The panoramic view of a poverty-stricken town
    Strewn with antennas,
And the yellow-toothed young polyglots
    Who picked at my pockets
    And offered to make babies with me.

But what of tenderness?

The tenderness of Tangier surfaced
From its allure and mystery,
Its beautiful blue water
    That served as backdrop to
    White stucco buildings
    And endless golden sand.
It emerged in a restaurant
    With bright ceramic-tile mosaics,
    Elaborate geometric patterns,
    And a view of the Strait of Gibraltar.
It surfaced with the kindness of
    A family that offered food
    When they could ill afford it,
And it leapt an ocean to provide
    Leather jackets for rich Americans
    Who never graced its shores.

**On the Return from Italy to Paris**

The wall of mist that smoked
From between those two green
Mountains cast a hush on all
Minds, making talk trivial
And hearts ingenuous.
The train continues even now
With the roll of that air
Breathing into each word
Its soulful sigh of morning
Tempests that enrage man-gods
Who shrink and shudder in
Denial of such muted verdancy.
I wish that mist, though dimmed
By celluloid and human frailty,
Could touch me again
And breathe these words
Into glorious peaks.

## High Bridge

Swirling water flows around
Smooth rocks with high watermarks.
Bleached, white trees form
Partial bridges that leave impressions
Of completeness.
Here and there is a fly fisherman
Wading in insulated rubber
But catching no trout today
Not even Bud who uses his
Inchworm fly
As he watches other green inchworms
Falling from a sky
Blanketed by trees.
And there is Tara,
Delicately balanced
On moss-covered globes,
Racing back and forth
Into the water
And off to some bushes
To explore territorial deposits
In this green dome.
I exchanged gifts with the river:
A piece of shredded lettuce
Caught among the rocks by the shore,
And the green smudge on my jeans,
Imprinted when I fell short of the rock
That jutted so uninvitingly
From the cold water
That climbed up my leg.
We consecrated this place
As ours to revisit
When we are so moved to
Sublime, lazy wetness.

**The Other Grand Canyon**

We descend the trail
Of ferns
As baby turkeys scatter
At our feet.
The mother, in torment,
Drives us away
And disappears
As we descend to Trout Run,
Disrupting the solace of
Pistol-bearing campers
Who catch hapless trout
In water that pours
From steel culvert pipes.

**On the Road to Mann Lodge**

As green treetops
Pass over my head
And reveal a blue,
Cloudless sky,
I am carried forth
To another waterfall,
Dark and verdant
Beneath a vertical drop.
Slanted rows of trees
Scream from
Mountaintops
And their
Leaves blur before me.
Here and there
Is a desecration of the land
Electric and phone wires —
Reminders that
Demanding voices
Can still be heard
Though no one present
Cares to listen.

**Cedar Run Inn**

The sitting room is a cacophony
Of oak, brass, tintype photos,
Marble, and a collection of videos
For the Ancients.
A sugar-water substance
At alternate windows
For hovering hummingbirds
Provides entertainment for the Moderns.
The waitress syllabicates
The four-star menu
That allows no substitutes and
No chicken for the steak man to grill.

After a predetermined meal
We head upstairs
To a room with one hard,
One soft bed, and a window fan
That blows in planned odors
From the kitchen below:
Such a welcome respite
From steep climbs,
Wet rocks,
And slimy salamanders.

**Tennessee Wind Farm**

A high place of vertical beauty
Offers its dying pines
To newcomers who would
Divide this landscape
For a breathless view.
Chosen bodies whose
Limbs crash silently
Burden these pink elements
With gravesites too visible for rest.
Cool, enveloped darkness
Invites outside ingredients
To blend with
This green nakedness.
Such alien structures,
Though absorbed
And soothed by this passive
Stronghold, cannot
Leave behind the cemented cacophony
Of inferior places.

**Reflections in a Blue High-Rise**

Staring at blue glass,
I see a reserved
Presence of mind,
A friendship becoming
But never being,
Windows
Opening and shutting
In whispers that
No one can hear.

In a stiff winter coat,
She blocks the breeze,
Smiles with wonder,
And pauses with fear
At the newness
And the distant
Distance between two
Glass panels moving slowly
Towards each other.

I see ninth-grade
Visions of me
In her blue reflection
Upright panels all
Construed to be
Properly placed,
And I look only
For the cracks
So her glass
Will explode and fall
On the chapel below.

**Gina I, II, III**

Gina I

I think of you,
Locked safely in your vault.
But who keeps
You from you?
If you could unzip the membrane
And walk through
The walls of your eyes
You could be free.

Gina II

In her trick-or-treat
Outfit of gloom
She glides through the labyrinth,
Surreally taking course
With the other lives
That bump into hers
In the hallway.
She needs a broom
For sweeping
And for flying,
For weeping
And for dying
And for smashing pumpkin faces.

Gina III

This sad girl
Inspires me;
Her words raise me
From her depths.
Feeding off her carcass,
I leave enough
For the vultures
Who will say
Bad things
About her black
Dresses and
Tresses and
Eyes that
Face west always,
Eclipsed by
Voices beckoning her
To grave places.

**Mono Lake**

Ansel Adams
"VII Plate I"

A study of contrasts
And shades born of
Surreal eyes,
Delimited only by
The commonness of viewers
Who partake vicariously
In this visual feast
Of white, stark limbs
Illuminated as twisted
Clumps of veiny extremities
At the edge of
A sea of fog.

**Yosemite from Ansel's Lens**

The lines in the photo
Startle the senses;
They soothe both the depths
And the surface
Of a soul
That scales the monolith.
Thin reeds, glass-like,
Melt into shades
Muted, yet crystalline.
Knotty wood chunks,
Dead before the lens,
Reappear, alive.

Such dark fronts for
Soft, grey backgrounds.

Such a suchness of beyond.

**"La Rochelle 1896"**

Crooked, lifeless sails
Top slanted boats
In a maze of wet,
Shale-like surfaces.
A splotched sky
Filters through the
Mist of dark wood
That beckons sailors
To untwist and unbend
Lifeless structures,
Opulent in their simplicity.

**"Venetian Patina"**

Barbara Taylor Hall
Painted the abstract
I saw at a show and bought
After it toured and won awards.

I had to have it

Because the rich
Rust-colored hues
Reflect the ancient
Buildings of Venice and
The oldest part of my soul
Before and after happiness

Because the off-white swirling circles
Towards the bottom
Reflect the gyre
That is my life.

Other lines
Are straight
Like my mathematical poems
Like the lines coming at me
From inadequate men
Like the screams
That still haunt me
On sleepless nights.

The splotches of color
Are a softer version
Of the horror
I feel when I see cellular ghosts
Drawing me back
To an unwelcoming mother's womb.

This painting is the geometry of my being;
It is at once rigid, soft, and mysterious,
Though it has a beauty
That has since vanished from my mirror.

**Bubbles Trail**

Near the end of the trail
Around Jordan Pond
In Acadia, there is
A seeming avalanche of boulders
That defaces the side of one
Of the Bubbles.

On the way up,
I followed a wife
Who lingered behind
To keep an eye on me.
I followed her footsteps
As my legs and feet,
Balanced on huge rocks,
Sought ground
But found little among the
Looming granite figures.

I was breathless and scared
But determined to
Mirror her way to the top.
The ascent was difficult;
My camera hung heavily from my neck,
My fingers balanced painfully on boulders,
And my body wavered unsteadily
As I cursed the metal lenses, the arthritic fingers,
And the Gabapentin haze.

It was the descent I really dreaded
I always have
But she would be there to
Guide me to a qualified calm.
I asked midway to the top
If I could follow her down,
And suddenly,
Out of this winged Siren's mouth
Came a dirge of a thousand volts,
"Oh, we're not going down.
We're taking another trail at the top."
Breathe....
I told myself I was not going to die
That day on a trail called Bubbles.

This newly-demonized woman
Became haloed once more by
Flagging down a woman
Whose grandchild would lead me to
The Promised Land.
All I had to do was follow
The young girl who plotted her course
Down the mountain in flip flops.
I mirrored each step,
Placed my feet in her path
And never raised my eyes
To face my fear.

From a distance, the twin mountains
Look like Bubbles,
But the real ones are the granite boulders
That slid down this mountain over time,
Disguising the trail and
Making this hike a mysterious
Maze of monoliths.

**Full Circle Farmhouse**
*Dedicated to Michele and George*

The acrid residue of smoke
Came to rest in our passageways
As we walked through the hull
Of the old farmhouse,
Sidestepping fallen sculptures
Of black wood and twisted metal.

The house survived the
Civil War and
Inserted itself
Into the union
Of a cast iron wood stove
And a thin wall of cement.
Wood curled and glowed
Behind the wall for years
Until it finally said,
"Enough."

The irony of the name
Of the farm
Escaped no one.
A new beginning
Would lay to rest
The pets, photos,
Mementos, and history
That expired that day
In a haze of smoke.

The aftermath reminds me
Of an old sonnet,
A glowing fire being consumed
By that which nourished it,
And lives emerging from ashes,
Coming full circle.

**Fish Pond**

You slowly submerge
The plastic bag
Into the pond
As confused goldfish swarm one side
And later join their terminal associates
Like translucent gladiators going off to war.

Spending most of the day
Under a large, flat slate,
They emerge
To eat the floating, green strands
And nibble the felt blanket
That clings to the rock bed.

Each day, another one leaves;
Some float away from their comrades,
Some find themselves
In the belly of a raccoon,
While others stay to solve the mystery
Of the deadly pond
Only to become a deeper part of it.

After the last sacrifice,
The soothing sound of water,
The sunlight on the upper falls,
The tentacles of lily blossoms,
And the occasional bird bathing
Against the backdrop
Of Hogback Mountain
Form a soulful symphony
At this watery tomb.

**Browntown Valley**

Ancient, eroded mountains
Host clouds that move eerily
Below the ridge line;
Transparent swatches of cotton
Meander to the northwest,
Leaving behind blue skies,
Green hills, and rounded peaks.

"The Crawling Eye" of 50s sci-fi
Does not emerge—
No fiction
Just science
And poetry in the movement
Of these serpentine clouds
And the disappearance
And reappearance
Of farmlands carved
Out of foothills,
Golden geometric forms
Against the greens and browns
Of Autumn.

Browntown Valley
Cushions and repels storms
That used to spread over me
And inside of me
In the harsh flatlands
That spun funnel clouds
Of Jersey judgment.

**The Glow**

In late afternoon,
When the sun is low in the sky
Yet visible above the mountains,
There is a glow
That accents the white bark of the sycamore trees
And highlights the earthen hues
Of the boulders that mark our property.

It is my favorite time of day
Despite reading that optimists prefer sunrise.

I have never feigned optimism;
I have worn my fatalism
And my pessimism towards life
As a badge of dishonor.

And yet, I am calmed and soothed
By this time of day;
All turmoil melts into the setting sun
And I can smell the aroma of dinner on the stove.

Life is good
Perhaps
Life is difficult
Yes
But still
At this time of day
I am grateful for the glow.

Thank you for reading
*A Consecration of the Wind.*
If you enjoyed this work, please consider leaving a review for it.

# About the Author

Raised in Middletown, New Jersey, Joanne Cherefko has spent her adult life in public education, from teacher to administrator to school board member, instilling a love and understanding of poetry in students.

She began writing poetry as a young girl, finding her voice in college, and creating her most complex, angst-ridden poetry after experiencing a grave personal loss. Her most recent poems shed a softer light on the demons of her past and reflect a clear departure from her earlier expressionist style.

Since 2007 Joanne has been creating and presenting poetry seminars at Mountain Vista Governor's School (MVGS) and local high schools in Warren County, Virginia. She is currently a visiting poet at Warren County High School and MVGS.

She enjoys researching challenging poets such as Wallace Stevens and Elizabeth Bishop in order to formulate thought-provoking questions that lead students to a critical analysis of poems they would otherwise never read, understand, or appreciate.

Joanne's hobbies are collecting and listening to music ranging from classic rock to contemporary alternative; photography; traveling; camping; hiking; researching poems to teach; writing poetry; cuddling with her dogs; and growing old with the love of her life, her devoted husband Bud.

Connect with Joanne

at www.joannezarrillocherefko.com

Made in the USA
Middletown, DE
24 January 2019